25 Days To A Better Marriage

Simple, Honest Advice From 37 Years of Real Life, Love, and Lessons

KIM ANSPACH

Foreword by Rob Anspach

25 Days to a Better Marriage
Simple, Honest Advice From
37 Years of Real Life, Love
and Lessons

Produced by: Anspach Media
Cover by: Freddy Solis

ISBN: 979-8-9926296-7-5

Disclaimer: This book is designed to give the reader general information on the subjects contained herein. It is offered with the understanding that the authors and publisher do not guarantee any specific future results. The authors are not rendering professional advice on specific facts or matters and, accordingly, assume no liability whatsoever in connection with its use.

Table of Contents

Foreword

By Rob Anspach

Yeah… I'm the guy.

The one she's been married to for over three decades. The one who's been on the receiving end of the love, the patience… and yeah, the occasional well-earned argument.

So if you're wondering whether any of what you're about to read actually works in real life… I'm your proof.

And let me be clear… we didn't get here because we had it all figured out.

We got here because we didn't quit.

Marriage isn't easy.

Anyone who tells you it is either just got started or isn't paying attention.

There are good days, great days, and days where you're wondering what the hell just happened. That's part of it.

What Kim has done in this book isn't write some polished, clinical, "this is how you should act" kind of guide. She's taken real moments, real lessons, and real experiences… and put them into something you can actually use.

And if you know her, this won't surprise you.

She says what she means. She feels everything deeply. And she's not afraid to call things out for what they are… even if it's messy.

Especially if it's messy.

That's why this works.

Because marriage is messy.

It's not built on perfection. It's built on showing up, day after day, choosing each other… even when it's hard, even when you don't feel like it.

Some of the things in this book will make you laugh. Some might hit a little too close to home. And some might make you stop and think, “Yeah… we need to work on that.”

Good.

That means it’s doing exactly what it’s supposed to do.

If you take anything from these pages, take this… small things matter more than big ones. The little conversations, the small gestures, the decision to listen instead of reacting… that’s where real change happens.

I’ve seen it. I’ve lived it.

And somehow, through all of it, we’re still here.

Still married. Still laughing. Still figuring it out as we go.

So don’t expect perfection from this book.

Expect honesty.

And if you’re willing to apply even a few of these ideas, don’t be surprised if your relationship starts to feel a little stronger… a little closer… and maybe even a little more fun again.

Alright… I've said enough.

I'll let her take it from here.

Introduction

By Kim Anspach

When I first started this little venture, it was simply a fun thing to do on Facebook for my friends. I wasn't planning on ever taking it any further.

Then I realized how much they all enjoyed it, so I thought maybe someday when my kids were older and I had more time. So, I printed it out and put it in a copy book for safe keeping.

Here I am 12 years later rewriting and adding to the original tidbits of practical advice I have gathered over my 37 years of being married.

Yes, to the same man!

Some of my advice may seem silly or even too simple to work. But relationships don't have to be complicated.

Starting from scratch, with the simple, may be just what you need. Sometimes just going back to basics, even remembering why you first fell in love, can bring new light while rushing those wonderful feelings and memories back to the surface.

Even if you are in a marriage that needs no help at all, this may just be a funny little anecdotal book to make you laugh and help you understand you aren't in it alone!

While I refer to this book being for married couples, I do believe it would also be good for those who are looking to form a good relationship who are still in the dating phase of life. It may even help you to understand what you want in a healthy relationship.

This is 25 days of practical advice that you could sit down and read all at once OR you could take one day at a time and really reflect on what I've said.

I believe the second way to read it is going to be the most helpful. I am happy to have written some of my personal opinions and observations for you and hope it brings you closer as a married couple.

Marriage- a few thoughts and some practical advice

I've been thinking a lot about what I have to offer others… well here it is … Experience!

Yep, it's that simple… Experience!

Christmas was 25 days away and I was married 25 years when this all began…

So, I thought I'd impart some of that knowledge on my friends and the world.

People ask me all the time 'what's the secret to being married so long.'

There is NO secret!

But in the next 25 days (if you read a chapter a day) I'm going to share with you 25 of my ideas on what may make a difference.

Understand I am not a counselor or person of any 'schooled authority' on the subject.

This is all about my practical and personal experience.

Chapter 1

An Act of God

"Though one may be overpowered, two can defend themselves. A cord of three strands is not quickly broken."

– Ecclesiastes 4:12

Our being married SO long is the will of God. Because God knows if it was ALL up to us, it would not work!

Why?

Because men and women are so different!

At least my husband and I are SO different!

There are many ways to go from here but I'm keeping it simple today… God must be the center of your love because without Him love does not exist… think about that…. God IS love therefore in any relationship, He must come first and be a part of it.

So how do we implement this God thing?

With each other… for each other… for your relationship and all the weaknesses in it ~ Prayer!

Pray for your failings, pray for encouragement, and pray for resiliency in your marriage.

Pray individually and together.

At first praying together may seem weird if you don't do it… keep it simple.

Start with "God thank you for the love we share. Amen."

God isn't complicated why does prayer have to be… it doesn't!

As you learn to pray in your relationship, the prayers will grow as you do. "God help us to have patience with each other on goods days and bad, help us by strengthening our hearts and minds to deal with our daily trials, and always nurture our faith and marriage molding us with your divine perfection.

In Your glorious hands all things are good. Amen."

This is vital for the health of your relationship because it creates personal intimacy and increases trust.

The bible says, “For where two or three are gathered in my name, there am I with them.” Matthew 18:20.

Praying together creates the foundation to an awesome love!

God bless you all and your marriage!

Marriage Takeaway:

- Put God at the center of your marriage, not just your problems
- Pray together, even if it feels awkward at first
- A strong marriage is built on faith, not just feelings

Chapter 2

Listening

"Most people do not listen with the intent to understand; they listen with the intent to reply."

– Stephen R. Covey

Everyone talks about communication being the key to a successful marriage. This is true.

But how many actually say how that's done? How do we communicate: listening, feeling, understanding, affection, facial expression, body language and actually talking to one another. Those are a lot of ways to communicate!

No wonder it's difficult!

And it's all happening at the same time…yikes!

Let us talk about listening. This is HUGE!

Proper listening entails ALL of your being- without distraction…. Let me reiterate- without distraction!

In our society this is very difficult! I think at times all our technology has made us all a bit ADD.

We constantly have to be doing something.
I know I do…lol but I've always been this way!

I was raised in a time without such technology so being active was natural because we never had screen time. It was natural to put everything aside and pay attention.

So, to truly listen we have too… sit with each other somewhere quiet without anything else distracting us.

Hard, I know, but you have to find your special place and time to listen to one another properly. Look at each other so you can see their facial expressions and watch their body language. This helps you to understand the intent of what your loved one is saying.

But as a listener- No talking! For now…open your heart and clear your mind of everything else but the person before you.

Remember that they love you and this means all of you the good and the 'in progress' parts as well.

They have no ill intent toward you and your goal is the same...to Love one another completely. This is where remembering God is the center of that Love (yesterday's topic) makes it easier to open up to the true beauty of the love your spouse has to offer you.

We build up so much crap in our minds that it's important to forget all the shit and just open up to the love. Yes, this is a Huge and a Difficult part of Listening because we have to be Open to listen. We listen with our minds, spirit, and ears! So much going on all at once.

Ok. We've opened our hearts, opened our minds and now comes the actual listening. Without thinking of everything else you need to be doing, just focus on the words flowing from your lover's mouth because at this moment in time nothing else is more important than what he/she is saying.

Truly, Just Listen!

And Be Open to what is being said... it's Important!

And please don't jump in with comments or be defensive.

Be patient your turn is coming next, and you will want them to give you that same respect.

With practice you can be an awesome listener.

And to say all this, doesn't mean I'm perfect at it either...

I'm a definite work in progress!

Love you all~ hope this brings you closer to that which you seek...

An Awesome Love!

God bless!

Marriage Takeaway:

- Give your spouse your full attention… no distractions
- Listen to understand, not to respond
- Respect their voice the way you want yours respected

Chapter 3

Talking Through Our Feelings

"Feelings are much like waves—we can't stop them from coming, but we can choose which ones to surf."

– Jonatan Mårtensson

In the previous chapter we started talking about communication through listening... key to a successful marriage.

Now let's reflect on Feelings...
and we have SO many of those don't we?!

It doesn't matter if you are male or female we all have feelings. We all experience sadness, joy, frustration, and so many complicated emotions.

Sometimes it takes some understanding of ourselves to know why we react to things the way we do. This is where personal reflection can help.

Reflect through prayer or times of silence.

To generalize, which I do often and is not meant to offend those who don't fit into my 'categories', women may be more emotional and as emotional as we are, men may hold it in and get angry. Not that we don't all get angry and experience those emotions at times but as genders go that's my experience.

What can we do to help our relationships with this understanding that we all have feelings?

Let's work with what we've got.

No, don't use our powers against each other! Understand that we are different and if we both do that, we can work with our strengths and sensitivities. You know your partner well enough to know how they'll react to any given predicament. So, try to be compassionate towards one another and always remember this person before you, loves you with all their heart and soul.

Remembering that will help you to be more kind and loving. Avoid pushing their buttons, no matter how much it entertains you!

Let's not cry or pout just because we don't get what we want or get furious cause something doesn't go our way...talk it out! The dialogue should go as such, "Honey, this really upset me because… or this is really important to me because..." and truly listen don't jump in to defend your territory or position in the matter.

Our emotions Are Not tools to be used against one another... God made us women emotional, and men can't stand when we cry, because God wanted them to be sensitive to us. This is not to be used as a weapon ladies!

With as strong as they can be, we need men to defend us from brute force...lol. They enjoy helping us in this manner… just let them do it! This is not saying we aren't forces to be reckoned with on our own. It's just letting them be men! That's a good thing!

Now let's talk about the anger side of it...
this is a defense mechanism.

As we use our emotions men grunt and holler at times. It's how they were made, so let's be a little sensitive to that fact. They can't always help it, and we don't want them to calm down so much they act like women...do we...NO, of course not! As well, don't let the fact that they do all this keep us from being honest with them. I know there are times when you know they are going to holler if you tell them (whatever); instead, don't tell them when they're angry already. Let us choose a better time, That Day, to be honest.

Don't jump on it as soon as he comes home from work and is already mad about the day. Let him fume a while. Give him a hug and wait for his feeling to settle. Then maybe it's time.

It is essential to learn how to subdue our inner beast and work through our feelings of anger. Sometimes we need to just walk away from a situation for a moment, take a few deep breathes, and calm ourselves before returning to the scene. This way we don't lash out at one another and say things we don't mean, or we will regret saying.

Having said all that... Men, don't yell when you are simply trying to talk~ calm the voice. Women want to feel respected and loved. This helps us to feel heard and that is so important for women. You will be rewarded for your restraint… trust me!

What place does anger have in a relationship?

Well sometimes anger happens but it's our job to make sure the anger isn't displaced. Is our spouse the reason for our feelings?

Let's be real… we all come with a past and that baggage is real. If it's our baggage creeping in, what do we do with it? Betrayal happens too. I wish that wasn't the case but if it's a betrayal, how do we work past that?

Talking through it, is the only way past whatever is happening. Look deeply at your relationship. This is not easy and will take time!

Truly dissect what's happened and why. There's always a why… some kind of disconnect in your marital happiness.

This is why you need to talk about everything. Be patient with yourselves!

Sometimes we do need a third party to help us work through our trials.

Therapy is an option but if that isn't your cup of tea, there are other options. A friend could be someone to lean on in your time of need if they are someone who has good in-site, has your best interest at heart- truly, loves you as a couple, and is a good person themselves. Anyone else just won't do! Maybe a mentor couple who can guide you through your trials. You need someone who wants to support your relationship and won't try to end it! A priest or pastor are readily available for this too.

There are times we just need to learn coping skills.

Anger Management isn't just a funny movie; it's a real choice to learn how to manage these feelings if it comes to that. At first learning skills to deal with anger may feel strange. But once you use them often enough, it will seem like second nature.

This is the hardest thing for most people... to forgive!

Forgiving someone who hurt us does not mean what they did was acceptable. It simply means that you will not hold that anger in your heart. So, in retrospect you are releasing that pain of what happened and giving it to God to deal with.

This will lighten your heart!

To reiterate we all have feelings...
Let's understand that simple fact when we are talking with one another!

I pray this helps us to understand each other’s difference, embrace them and make you better spouses and the best of all Great Lovers!

Hoping you get everything you want from your relationships.

God Bless You All.

And Remember God Must be the Center of your love!

Marriage Takeaway:

- Be honest about your feelings without attacking
- Choose the right time for difficult conversations
- Work through emotions… don’t weaponize them

“Marriage doesn’t fall apart overnight…

it fades when we stop paying attention.”

Chapter 4

Facial Expressions

& Body Language

"The most important thing in communication is hearing what isn't said."

– Peter Drucker

While we are trying to perfect the skills of listening and talking through the multitude of feelings we all have, we must consider our outward expressions.

How is the face expressing our feelings?
What does our body language say about the present situation?

These are questions to keep in mind.

This tells your lover if you are open to the conversation or closed off. Being closed off means you are not going to truly hear what is being said.

The best course of action when seriously discussing issues with your spouse is to sit across from them, watch your posture, sit up straight, don't fidget or focus on anything else but the present moment. Have a relaxed body and look into their eyes.

You are not in front of the firing squad even though sometimes that it is how it feels.

So, demonstrate a calm attitude. It has to start somewhere so it may as well start with you.

With some people it's easy to understand how they feel because of their facial expressions. I am a prime example of this. Everything I feel goes straight to my face.

These days we hear about micro expressions. These are involuntary short expressions which reflects our true feelings. We cannot control these expressions. So, this is not what we are talking about here.

Like I've said before, I'm not a counselor or therapist or any such thing therefore I won't get into those levels of facial expression. You'd need another book for that!

The expressions we are talking about are the ones that stay on your face… like glaring at your spouse because you don't like what they are saying.

That's just one example of a multitude of expressions.

Remember you will get your turn in the conversation. Instead of glaring at your spouse maybe just sit there with a thoughtful expression… listening intently.

It will be your turn to get your ideas across soon enough.

After that you can agree on a compromise.

But in the meantime, you don’t want to be sitting across from each other glaring and hating on your lover.

That is no way to hold yourself in any discussion.

Let’s love each other better by being kind and respectful even when we are not happy with a problem.

Give one another the respect you deserve through your expressions of your body language and face.

God is in the middle of all that… now soften that brow! I hope this helps a little in yourself awareness and brings you closer to your ultimate love for one another!

God be with you!

Marriage Takeaway:

- Your body language speaks before your words do
- Stay open and calm during conversations
- Show respect—even when you don't agree

“It’s not the big moments that define your marriage…
it’s the small ones you repeat every day.”

Chapter 5

Affection

"Where there is love there is life."

– Mahatma Gandhi

With fear that I may be boring you, today I'm going to talk about the most pleasurable form of communication….

Affection...bow chicka wow wow…

No, it's not all about sex but it does come into play at some point...lol.

Whatever you do Never hold back on your affections. There are appropriate times and places of course. But if you want too, for no apparent reason, just grab your spouse and give ‘em a smoocharoo- then go for it!

Spontaneity makes heat...Yes… heat and passion.

We don’t want our relationship to get dull and boring. Ever!!!! Heat and Passion are a necessity!

Affection comes in many forms as well. Of course, hugs, kisses, touching etc., but have you ever thought of affection as more than just that... like flirting, a sexy glance, a text message saying, "just thinking about you" or "can't wait to get home and...". Just make sure that message is being sent to the correct person.

You don't want your mom opening a message that says something a bit naughty. Can you imagine? Ha, Ha!

Affection is any form of attention that is directly related to your bonding as a married couple.

And don't say well I don't like PDA (public displays of affection) - that's horse shit! Just show her you love her and who cares if the world sees it~ big deal!

The world needs more love not less.

Hold one another's hand as you walk down the street. Make sure to kiss each other goodbye and hello at the beginning and end of your day. Tell each other you love one another. Words spoken, along with action, means so much! Take her dancing and show the world she is on Your arm. This will definitely spice it up and trust me, she will show you later just how much!

I don't know how it is for men, but for women our emotional nurturing through affection outside the bedroom is directly related to how we love our husbands in the bedroom. Think about that for a moment.

Say it slowly… *Women's emotional nurturing through affection outside the bedroom is directly related to how we love our husbands in the bedroom.*

That is so important I had to say it twice and italicized it. Get the hint!

With all this spontaneity you will have more passion for one another. This is my hope for you. Passion! Now we can add the sex.

There's not much to be said here because most couples know how this works. One thing I should say is to be patient with one another even in this department. As we know from all the ads, things don't always work the way they should, no matter your gender. This is where patience can be a great benefit!

Whatever you do, don't schedule your love making because then it becomes routine and may start feeling like a chore. It definitely should not be that...lol.

Just do it, when and where you want (of course not in public...lol… have some respect!).

But be spontaneous!
Have as much as you can stand!

Yep, I said that! With God as the center of your life and love this department becomes even more fabulous! I am Catholic and my religion considers this act between husband and wife a Sacrament and part of our commitment to one another.

Our duty if you will! So, let's Not disappoint God!

With all we have talked about so far... praying, listening, feelings, and now affection you should hopefully be getting a few ideas on what you may need in your life together.

I just hope a small bit of this helps you or just makes you laugh your ass off!

Either way, I'm Good!

God Bless!

Marriage Takeaway:

- Show affection often… not just when it’s convenient
- Keep spontaneity alive in your relationship
- Emotional connection drives physical connection

Chapter 6

Disagreements

(discuss rules of arguing)

"In a relationship, it's not about who wins the argument, but how you protect the connection."

– Tony Gaskins

Hopefully, we are not calling it Random thoughts of a crazy lady...lol.

What I am so good at, is this topic...Arguments.

Yes, we are all guilty of this one, but I am Queen! lol ...
My Poor Hubby!

At this time in my life and some of you will totally be able to relate cause you're in it, just past it, or soon to be there.

Hormones...Why did God make our hormones the way he did? I'm a nut case I tell you. If it wasn't bad enough to have hormonal changes in puberty, then pregnancy, and now Menopausal changes.

What was God thinking?

Did he want us to drive men insane?!

LOL! If it wasn't hard enough being married and understanding one another, now this! Men are lucky in the fact they don't share in our changes cause if they did, we'd all be done for!

I'm normally sweet and loving but then something gets into my head and BAM… Medusa comes out!

And Rob is saying "What is going on with you!" And I rant and argue and go about like a tornado... maybe this topic should be called hormones...lol.

The constant prayer I pray is "God get this devil outa my head". I can feel it picking and picking. Anyone else feels like this? I know these are hormonal changes, but I feel like I'm under attack which on a spiritual plain~ I am.

Did you know woman carry out God's great plan of procreation and the devil hates us for this? Yes, men we can't do it without you but the actual pain in childbirth is a true sacrifice, and El diablo hates us for that. So, he does attack us!

Growing up in my house arguing was a form of communication and it doesn't usually produce a good outcome. So right off the bat I knew the art form well. It has taken me Years not to be so argumentative but boy when I lapse it's a *doozy!*

(Sometimes guys when we get like this especially in our hormonal states just gently grab us and show us some darn affection. It Will most likely calm **our nuttiness.** Unless she's a fighter- then maybe don't.)

Rules of engagement are necessary as in any strategy of warfare. Ground rules are expected just like in the game Stratego.

At some point of your marriage, you should have mapped out what is allowed and not allowed in these times of disagreement just like the Geneva Convention.

Doing this ahead of time, not during an argument will help you to think before you speak.

Never bring up past issues only focus on the present.

Save past issues for another discussion if those weren't already cared for. When arguments happen, because they will, remember this person before you loves you. He or she does not want to make you feel isolated or attacked.

God is in your hearts, relationship, and is guarding you with His ultimate love!

So, hold each other and remember you are protected.

Cherish each other, as God cherishes you in your faults, weakness, and all that you are.

May His love flow between you always!

Forgive one another and don't forget to ask each other for forgiveness. Being proud doesn't help anyone!

Praise your lover for the patience they demonstrate especially on their crazy days.

God Bless you all and I will pray for you!

Marriage Takeaway:

- Set rules for how you argue before you argue
- Stay focused on the present… not past baggage
- Protect the relationship, not your ego

Chapter 7

Express It

"How do you know he loves you…

if he doesn't show you?"

– Enchanted

It's not enough to have all these feelings of love and romance. We need to Express it! Have you ever seen the movie "Enchanted"?

If you haven't, I suggest you do because it is exactly how it should be; maybe a little over the top, but you'll understand. There is a line in it that goes "How does she know you love her... how does she know?".

Well, that's simple...she/he doesn't unless you express it...and I'm not talking about sex. This has to be done outside the bedroom people. Women especially need to be emotionally nurtured, time spent, a hug or kiss as you pass.

These things do build up to fulfillment of heart.

She needs to know she's on your mind constantly. Yes, ladies that's how men's minds work. They think of us often. It's these little things that matter the most!

Don't over complicate it. If you aren't used to saying "I love you" start and end your day with these words. But seriously, don’t make it seem insincere or like a chore. That'll just piss her off! After getting used to that, learn to complement each other. "Honey, you look so pretty today." And be specific! "I love looking in your eyes. They tell me when you're happy."

Not only women love to be complimented, men do too!

When your loved one goes out of their way to do something for you, recognition is appreciated. “Thanks, honey, for doing to dishes. I was dreading that after my long day."

Make them feel appreciated when you notice they have done something for you. Say something...don’t be a jerk and say later. "Yeah, I noticed I just didn’t say anything":

Really? That's not gonna get you any points. And the point of all this is to become better spouses, friends, and lovers.

Guys you want as much as you can handle from her. This is huge with women!

Women, men eat it up when you compliment what they've done for you and get hurt feelings, which looks like anger, when you don’t notice.

So, this is Not gender specific.

Take notice People and Express it. Tell each other everything you feel cause if you don’t say it...we don't know it!

May God be with you, in your hearts, and the center of all your relationships.

God Bless you all!

Marriage Takeaway:

- Say what you feel… don’t assume they know
- Compliment and appreciate each other often
- If you don’t express it… they don’t feel it

Chapter 8

Thoughtfulness

"Small things done with great love will change the world."

– Mother Teresa

With the Christmas we find ourselves busier than ever. Some of us are so busy with everyday life we would like to forget all about it.

Please keep in mind the holiday Isn't about you! It is Not about the commercialism of materialistic possessions either. It IS about the birth of Jesus Christ our Lord and Savior; the Love He brought to the world and finally our eternal salvation.

Now you may be thinking, What does this have to do with thoughtfulness?'...

With God as the center of our marital love this holiday is a prime example of a time we can remember our spouse and do something extra special for them.

Don't say you do...I'm not buying it! LOL.

If you actually are a thoughtful person, you won't mind taking a little extra time to think of something to do for your lover. It doesn't have to require money or going shopping. Maybe you are just a terrible gift giver. Your spouse knows this by now! Start by helping out more with whatever they are bogged down with on a daily basis.

If the dishes are the chore that is their responsibility...do the dish for a week as a special gift or take the time to give him a foot massage. This is the time of the year your Love can be so much more, but it does require a little effort on your part.

Your relationship can only be as good as the time you are willing to put into it. So, let's not start thinking about what to do for our spouse on Christmas Eve....start Right Now!

Don't be a lazy lover... that's just sad!

May Christ find you all in good health and happiness this Christmas Season.

Hold each other tenderly Every Day and just be thoughtful to the other's needs!

May God's Blessings be upon you!

Marriage Takeaway:

- Thoughtfulness doesn't require money… just effort
- Pay attention to what your spouse needs
- Don't wait for special occasions… start now

Chapter 9

Patience

"Patience is not simply the ability to wait—
it's how we behave while we're waiting."
– Joyce Meyer

Practicing empathy for your spouse will help develop patience. This will aid you with conflict resolution, fostering compassion for one another, and in reducing misunderstandings.

Trying to appreciate your spouse and their feelings, gives them a sense they are understood while fostering a deeper connection. This helps us develop better emotional, mental, and physical health. Our overall well-being is relying on us making these connections within our relationship.

It is easy for me to remind myself to have patience with my kids young and adult, but when it comes to my husband, I have little left. So, I've been trying Very Hard to remind myself not to take the days stress out on him and to vow every day to be calm and patient with him.

Sometimes it means for me just taking a moment to respond with love or taking a deep breath or two, so I don't act with intolerance. The patience game is a tough one… but one day at a time and I assure you, it will get better.

For example: I am trying to calm my 2-year-old granddaughter because she didn't want me to brush her teeth. Now she is throwing herself all around and screaming- a full-blown tantrum.

Meanwhile my husband comes into the room trying to console her without understanding- it's a tantrum... she's not hurt! I am ready to boil over because he wonders what I've done to make this little sweetie cry…

Patience here looks like… a few deep breaths and calming myself so I don't scream at him… followed by a quiet 'please walk away!'

Sometimes that's all you got! It's like read the room buddy.

You too can learn to be patient with your spouse as I try very hard to be with mine.

One important thing to remember in all of this is...
Don't Bottle it Up!

If you do, the patience you have been trying to maintain, will be a farce and come bursting out one day.

Talk about all your feelings and don't 'avoid'.

That is not being patient... it's being dumb!

Sorry, no better way to say it!

Hold each other close and love each other the way God intended.

Enjoy the pure serenity of just being together. Good night and may God find you peaceful in your dreams.

God Bless!

Marriage Takeaway:

- Pause before reacting… respond with intention
- Don't take your stress out on your spouse
- Patience is practiced daily, not occasionally

Chapter 10

Quality Time

"To love someone is to give them your attention."

– Thich Nhat Hanh

It's most vital in our busy lives to Spend Quality Time Together!

Quality time means to dedicate specific time to interact with one another free from distractions to strengthen your emotional bonds by being fully present and attentive. This fosters trust and intimacy through shared experiences.

So, forget soccer practice, carting kids around for one night, or whatever life is throwing at you and just focus on the two of you.

Making the time is hard but a true necessity!

You both deserve it! You need at least one day per month, if not more, to really have bonding time. You can choose to go on date night, just have a weekly walk together, or star gazing time. It is not about spending money or going out. So don't let that hold you back. It's about having a day or evening where it's just the two of you strengthening your friendship.

If you can schedule for a weekend getaway, more power to you. That kind of time spent, can be a true game changer.

In the past my husband and I have taken dance classes at our local Rec Center. No, we still aren't very good, but we had a ton of fun... yes getting clotheslined was a part of it.

And while at the time I was very upset and vowed never to dance with him again, it would have been hilarious to watch it over the years in slow motion.

The class I will always remember was our belly dancing class. Yes, Rob set aside all his ideas of what a man should and shouldn't do and took a belly dancing class with me, just for shits and giggles!

He knew I'd get a charge out of it. It was a hoot!

Kudos to Rob for doing something just because I wanted too. LOL. And this is what it's all about!

It doesn't matter if one of you really aren't interested in said activity- sacrificing is a part of love...It was about the time we spent together.

It was time we had scheduled to get out of the house, away from other responsibilities, and to focus on each other. We had a fun time doing it.

So go spend a few precious or hilarious moments together.

We never know how much time we have so make it memorable!

May God be in the center of your hearts and marriage!

Marriage Takeaway:

- Make time for each other… on purpose
- Be fully present… no phones, no distractions
- Shared time builds stronger emotional bonds

Chapter 11

Stress

"Sometimes being there is enough."

– Colleen Hoover

We have all kinds of stressors in our lives, let's try to help each other deal with them. Some stress is from work, our environment, and let's be serious- family… just to name a few.

Simply taking the time to talk about it can help.

You may have to be the listener on this one. Your spouse doesn't need you to fix the problem! Just being a sounding board helps more than we sometimes understand. Finding solutions to help alleviate stress is good.

Maybe some changes need to happen if it's a constant issue.

For example, if I know my spouse had an awful day. Since I get home first, I make his favorite dinner, prep the kids to understand he needs quiet time, and make the house a destress zone (a beer may be involved).

If you know he can't stand the living room being a laundry dumping zone where folding happens… move it!

One less thing to cause an argument that day. This is Not an easy thing, but TRY is the word here.

Personally, sometimes I just come home and slump on the sofa on a difficult day, chill for a while and then if it's not better, a hot bath with a lavender bath bomb and some classic French music by Edith Piaf. That gives me time to calm myself and finish my day afterward.

My point here...We need to learn to recognize when our loved one is stressed and help if we can. At times it may mean taking on some of their responsibilities ourselves… a sacrifice I know but that's what this love thing is all about...Sacrificing for one another! Other times it may mean just letting them alone to deal with their own feelings. Some people need to work through things on their own.

Respect that process!

At the same time as adults, we need to learn what relaxes and de-stresses us so when our spouse asks what we need- we know how to answer that question.

May God Bless all your endeavors and may He help you to be closer to your spouse!

Marriage Takeaway:

- Sometimes your spouse just needs you to listen
- Be a place of peace—not more pressure
- Learn what helps each other decompress

Chapter 12

Sacrifice

"Love is not about how much you do, but how much love you put into what you do."

– Mother Teresa

It's only day 12 (if you're doing a chapter a day) and this one might the one that hits the hardest. Sacrifice is our topic for this chapter!

When we love one another there is always a degree of sacrifice... sometimes it may be a little like, "do I really have to get off this sofa to do that for you." … and some will be huge "that means I have to rearrange my entire days schedule."

For me it has become routine to sacrifice for my kids but the husband… I think for many years I had the attitude of "You're a big boy, do it Yourself."

Well, that is not too loving now, is it?! No, it's not! Shame on me! As the kids have grown, I have learned to say to them "You are a big boy/girl. Do it yourself." Now I don't feel so stressed and overwhelmed that I have one more person who demands of me.

As a mom this is huge...we get bogged down and totally stressed because we do for everyone else!

Well guess what~ tomorrow I'm getting a massage...yay me! Where is the sacrifice in that you say. The sacrifice wasn't mine this time- my husband sacrificed for me! Love It!

Sometimes you have to let others sacrifice for you... Stop being Wonder Woman for one day and let yourself have a relaxing day or at least an hour...lol. After that, yes, you will be running as usual. But for that moment... you can relax!

Are you wondering how this affects marriage? If you forget to take care of yourself, how can you take care of others and be that awesome wife or husband you want to be?! Occasionally, it may mean guys night, lunch with the girls, or a massage. But we have to get away from our normal routine and remember to love ourselves in this way. Time to decompress is vital!

Now I've gone a different direction with this than I expected to go, so let's redirect. As a loving married couple, you need to sacrifice for one another. That means many things, but the end result is awesome. And don't be afraid to let each other know when you have done something sacrificial. Not in a boastful way but you can say ‘guess what I did today?’ We can't appreciate what we don't know. Talk about everything. That's how you learn about each other while having less communication issues. Yes, all sacrifices don’t have to be announced but some of those will be in forms of prayer for one another.

With sacrifices most are little and God Bless you when they are huge! May God's love find you making more sacrifices for one another to increase the love you have for each other.

With God all things are possible! May His blessings be upon you!

Marriage Takeaway:

- Love requires giving… not keeping score
- Let your spouse take care of you too
- Take care of yourself so you can show up better

Chapter 13

Learn to Adore One Another

"Never stop dating your spouse."

– Dave Willis

With Christmas on its way you hear grown-ups say, "I'm not ready yet!" but kids are anxious and elated at the thought of how much longer until it will be here. We Adults need to be like kids again! Slow things down, if need be, but make life about looking forward too... (fill in the blank).

Whether it's the holiday, or a vacation, or date night out. Go chase an ice cream truck down the road. We NEED to have things to look forward to, like a child would.

How does this affect your married life you ask?

We need to get ourselves in the position that we look forward to time together. Be excited to get home from work and fall into each other’s arms. After being married 37 years the honeymoon period is Long Gone but you can get it back or rehab your married life, if you will.

How do you do this?

First, you have to miss each other. Secondly, each of you have too really want the same thing... a Wonderful marriage! It involves being SO honest with each other that it hurts at times and learning how to be affectionate all over again. This can be a gut-wrenching experience, but these conversations Need to happen.

Once you've done this the air will be cleared and healing begins leaving room for… Love to ignite. Ladies there is an on switch...if you haven't found it... find it...lol. Not getting any racier than that. Hint: it's tied to emotion! I spoke about it briefly in the topic of affection.

So how do we act like kids again with each other? Don't hold grudges, get rid of all the past shit ...deal with it, forgive it, and forget it! Sometimes it's a daily choice to do these things. Just keep on pushing toward forgiveness.

Little boys are great at this... mad one minute, friends the next. We adults must learn to do this. Ladies not so easy for most of us. We like to stew in it and hold a grudge all day and longer! Try very hard to learn a healthier attitude.

Express your love with small gestures. Bring home flowers or his favorite candy bar. The tiny things are often more memorable than the grande.

Be available to adore one another by appreciating the deep emotional connections you are making. Plan short vacations, date night, pizza n a movie in bed if you must. Any time… just so its time spent and its together. Even running errands, just the two of you, is Time Spent.

So, let's Refire Up your friendship and take the example of little kids on forgiving and making up!

May God always be the center of your hearts and love!

Marriage Takeaway:

- Never stop dating your spouse
- Let go of grudges… choose connection
- Make time together something you look forward to

Chapter 14

Apologizing

This should be short and sweet.

"Apology is the superglue of life."

– Lynn Johnston

No matter what, don't just let it go...Apologize!

Say the words “I am sorry!”

You need to humble yourself, forget your pride, and just consider your spouse’s feelings in all you do. For this reason, we should all get used to Apologizing. It's not easy but eventually when you get used to it... it becomes second nature!

Sometimes a simple "Will you forgive me?" will do but if it's a doozy make it extra special... flowers or something your spouse would consider special...tickets to a ball game...idk. You know each other best…make it a good one!

Along with this comes forgiveness.

We must get used to using these word and say, "I forgive you!"

Not saying by any means this will always be easy, but a spirit of forgiveness rests the soul and gives you a peaceful heart. Having this makes it so much easier to love one another.

Sometimes forgiving is a daily choice.

Not letting the anger creep into your head, yet again, is a daily choice.

With God as the center of your love, forgiveness is always possible because He invented it.

Love each other with openness and pureness of heart.

May God hold you in your times of struggles and keep you always in His graces!

Hold each other close and cherish your time together!

God Bless!

Marriage Takeaway:

- Say “I’m sorry” and mean it
- Forgive without keeping score
- Humility strengthens love

Chapter 15

Reality Check

"A happy marriage is the union of two good forgivers."

– Ruth Bell Graham

Yes, while we are talking about how to improve your love through your marriage it is important to remember... You are Not always going to be totally in-sync with one another.

You are going to have bad days...
And it Will be difficult to be loving and patient with one another.

In these cases, you have to figure out what works for you.

Maybe you need to walk away for a short time. But try your damnedest not to stew in it. When I stew in it...I come back with a vengeance...it's NOT pretty...I do Finally get heard but it causes Way too much stress. And we Do Not need this in our relationship!

Be sure to come back to the conversation with love and honesty.

I CAN'T SAY it any Louder...
Listen and Let your lover be heard!

If you aren't being heard in a relationship, it makes you feel like what you have to say is Not Important and just the opposite is true.

Everything you have to say IS Most Important!

So, make sure you let your spouse know this and give them the time to speak and Be Heard! Don't let this end your relationship and trust me when someone feels unheard it can lead to that. A person can only take so much and those feeling of inadequacy build up until you can't take it anymore.

If you don't understand what I'm saying here, listen to the song 'Speechless' sung by Naomi Scott. It talks about feeling trapped, unheard, and then breaking free not allowing the pattern to continue.

No one should ever feel this way in a loving relationship.

This means- Be a Good Listener!

At the same time talk… don’t be afraid to speak the truth. If you aren’t honest about this, your spouse will not know how you feel.

You are responsible in this circumstance to be brave and speak that truth. I am saying this out of personal experience… you are not alone in this!

This is where building intimacy helps us create the foundation of emotional connections and trust.

Open communication is key.

This at times will require both of you to be vulnerable; growth happens when we do this. All the time spent together engaging in activities, family time, laughter these all help foster connections on a personal, deep level.

In times of feeling out of touch with one another fall to the memories of good times and remember your love for one another.

Yes, this can be a challenge when you don’t feel close to each other.

While some days you may feel like you aren't being heard or in-sync with one another God is always listening.

Bend your knee in prayer!

Imagine the frustration He goes through with us...we just get a small dose of it from the ones we love!

Thank God He is in charge.

May God's love help you to build the foundations of intimacy needed for your marriage!

Peace and Love to you and yours!

Marriage Takeaway:

- You won’t always be in sync—and that’s normal
- Make sure your spouse feels heard
- Come back to love after every disagreement

“Love isn’t about being perfect…
it’s about choosing each other anyway.”

Chapter 16

Forgiveness

"Forgiveness does not change the past, but it does enlarge the future."

– Paul Boese

What makes Christmas Special to you?

For me it's the excited children who can't wait for Santa to arrive, the anticipation of people opening the presents I give to them, Christmas Eve Mass together as a family, and finally the true story of Christmas the birth of our Lord Jesus Christ!

Traditions: My Grandmother has always had a birthday cake topper that is gold with angels that spin by the heat of the candles. Along with this we sing Happy Birthday to Jesus. It will be the one thing I always remember. She Is still alive at 97 years old* but I'm appreciating her ideas while she is still here.

What does this have to do with marriage.

Her and my grandfather were a particularly good example for a loving couple who dearly cherished each other. We all need to have good examples to know how it should be done- right!
So, if you don't, go find one... Not tv couples...real ones!

My other set of grandparents were a hoot... they'd argue in front of us all the time. There was a story of my grandma chasing him with a butcher knife (I later heard the whole story and understood) but as they got older you could see all that was left was their friendship. In their late 90's my grandparents were sitting outside on my patio enjoying the day and grandad looked sweetly into grandma's eye and asked if he was a good husband. She turned to him and reassured him he was good to her. It was precious!

That influenced me in a dramatic way.

Because I knew things of the contrary and she chose to forgive his discretions.

This is what I'm always talking about... Let the shit lie, just love, and forgive each other!

Imagine what our relationships could be!

Stop just Imagining and make it a Reality!

Oh, What Love we could give one another... without expectation- kind, honest and pure!

With God in the center of all that, we could be SO much more!

Keep the Love of Christ in your hearts, on your mind, and in your marriage.

God Bless!

Marriage Takeaway:

- Let go of past hurts… even if it takes time
- Forgiveness frees you more than them
- Focus on what you're building, not what happened

**When I started this journey of sharing my thoughts my grandmother was 97 years, she passed at 101. That was 8 years ago.*

Chapter 17

Laugh Together

"Laughter is the closest distance between two people."

– Victor Borge

They say laughter cures what ails you!

Well, it may not cure everything but it sure will bring people together. Nothing makes people feel closer and more supported than when they have a hysterical encounter. Inside jokes and playfulness enhance a couple's emotional connection and adds to their shared story.

This makes it possible to dissolve issues that we were too proud to otherwise deal with. When your heart is light from laughter, it may be a suitable time to talk, and work throw things.

So how do you apply this to your marriage?

At some point in your relationship, you were able to make each other laugh otherwise you wouldn't have hooked up to begin with.

You need to find that laughter again.

Go out with friends, see a funny movie, and laugh about it later.

Whatever and wherever you make it happen~
it doesn’t matter...
just find the laughter in each other and enjoy yourselves as a couple.

See the beauty, the awkward silliness in yourself and your spouse.

Don't take yourselves so seriously!

In each other’s arms life should be light, joyful, and happy which has no place for work type seriousness...not most of the time any way!

May God find you always in each other’s arms and cherishing each other’s stupidity!

God Bless you all!

Marriage Takeaway:

- Don't take everything so seriously
- Create moments of joy together
- Laughter strengthens your connection

Chapter 18

Bending For One Another...

(No, Not Like That)

"Compromise is the best and cheapest lawyer."

– Robert Louis Stevenson

As we grow older, we look at ourselves in a different, more mature way than we did as kids.

We should strive to always make ourselves better... whether it is getting closer to God, improving our talents, becoming more patient etc.

With this understanding how do we apply this to our marriage?

We need to improve ourselves to make secure the oneness of our relationship with our spouse. In getting married the two become one; therefore, you become like one another and in this become one in love and all things.

That is why they say as we get old together, we take on the others personality and that is how it should be.

But how does a couple bend for one another?

We learn to value one another's perspectives by understanding there may be more than one solution to any given problem. Practicing compromise to find the solutions we need, strengthens our relationships helping both partners feel heard, and respected.

Finding the common ground, without compromising your values, that mutually benefits both you and your spouse.

I love when I see an old couple walking, holding hand and they seem so in tune with each other, like it's a dance and they are flowing so divinely in it.

"That", I say to Rob, "Is what I want us to be."

Together in Love and all that is us as a couple.

Hoping you get a little oneness with each other today.

God Bless and may your Love be divine!

Marriage Takeaway:

- Compromise without losing your values
- Respect each other's perspective
- Flexibility keeps the relationship strong

Chapter 19

Random Acts of Kindness

"No act of kindness, no matter how small, is ever wasted."

– Aesop

We think of these random acts hopefully all year long but more so at Christmas time.

How can we help others, even strangers?

But have you considered as well, random acts of kindness for your spouse?

We have our routines of everyday life but just out of the blue doing something totally sweet is very appreciated and quite unexpected… Leave a love note, make your significant other coffee, buy a small treat, or help with chores.

The sky is the limit… use your imagination!

Love notes are the best!

When my husband and I were first dating he used to leave notes for me on my parent's chalk board when he was hanging out with my brother.

Yes, he was my brother's friend first.

It was just the sweetest thing that really touched my heart. Sometimes they were silly, other times cute… but memorable.

This is the point… make memories that touch the heart!

Fast forward many years later… I was sitting at my son's karate class one night dreading of coming home to make dinner.

Now this next part almost gave me a heart attack....
We went home and what was sitting on the kitchen table... dinner and my husband standing there with a spatula in hand and smirk on his face.

What?! We had pancakes for dinner. Thank you, Rob!

I was So Happy! This never happens.

My husband does not cook!

So, think… What random acts of kindness can you do for your spouse today?

May you have God in your hearts and peace in your day...Love You all!

Marriage Takeaway:

- Surprise your spouse with small gestures
- Keep love alive in everyday moments
- It's the little things that are remembered most

Chapter 20

Humility

"Humility is not thinking less of yourself,

but thinking of yourself less."

– C.S. Lewis

Humility is defined as having a modest view of your importance. This does not mean you aren’t important. It means put others before yourself.

In our relationships we find ourselves being proud at times, feeling we must defend ourselves and our actions. Don't feel like that!

You’re not a kid anymore and your spouse is not your parent!

Remember your spouse loves you.

So now is the time to not only be patient but humble as well. Hear them out, take a few moments to contemplate what was said, and then talk. Think of them and then yourself.

It is not easy...having humility!

I found a quote online (madamenoir.com) that sums it all up!

"Love is a short word with many characteristics and meanings. It is often defined as patient, kind, not envious and it doesn't keep record of right or wrong. Out of all the varying attributes of love, there is one that is often overlooked and needs to be expressed more in relationships. That trait is humility. Being humble is the act and art of swallowing one's pride or minimizing one's ego. In relationships, many people fail to realize that humility and love go hand-in-hand, and in failing to recognize this, many people don't implement it within their relationship and in turn fail to display love at its best."

I couldn't have said it better myself... pray for humility!

Us Catholics have a beautiful prayer called the Litany of Humility. (You can find it online.)

It is the best prayer I know to help with personal growth. In coming closer to God, we understand the desires and fears that we need to shed from ourselves.

This prayer also helps us understand what graces to desire from the Lord.

Look it up… it's a beautiful prayer whether you are Catholic or not.

God Bless you in your relationship and in trying to be humble!

Marriage Takeaway:

- Put your spouse before your pride
- Listen before defending yourself
- Humility deepens love and respect

Chapter 21

Perseverance

"Love never fails."

– 1 Corinthians 13:8

Perseverance - doing something despite difficulty or whether success is delayed.

Love Never Ends.

Have you ever really been mad at someone?

Have you ever felt that you hate them?

I always said hate is such a strong word. Why?

Because it is. In order to hate someone, you had to have some love in your heart or feelings of some sort for that person. It doesn't come out of nothing.

In your marriage if you've gotten to this place of hatred, start with the following.

First, examine if that's truly what you're feeling?
Second, why are you feeling it?
Third, do you want to stay there and soak in the misery or would you rather get rid of all that hurt?

This is what hatred is… you've been wounded. Well… this is where change begins. Use all the skills you've learned in your relationship and work it through.

Talk it out sincerely, patiently, with kindness, with tenderness, and respect.
Decide together how you want to proceed, after it's all talked over and you've both said your peace.

Just keep working on things every day. Love doesn't just end. We get in the way of it! But it takes two dedicated people to work through the difficulties of marriage. Life happens to all of us. Families can be difficult plus so many other things and it all affects our marriage. Sometimes it tries to get in the middle of it. Don't let that happen!

Keep pressing on and get good counsel if needed. Can't afford therapy sessions? How about your priest or pastor? It's part of what they're trained for. Take full advantage of the help that is available to you. Don't be afraid to ask for guidance.

Now I’ve gone and made it all sad. Perseverance isn’t only in sad times or bad times. Good things happen from practicing this. Daily life can be overwhelming and sometimes just getting through the day is a challenge.

Honestly, with the practice of prayer and a good routine perseverance is possible. And getting all your days’ work done is possible too. Keep pushing forward. Just keep swimming, just keep swimming. Sometimes this may seem like what I’m writing is repetitious but that is how we get the concepts drilled into our head. We learn and improve by repetition so keep pushing forward.

God Bless...Be well my friends!

Marriage Takeaway:

- Keep working through the hard seasons
- Ask for help when needed
- Love is a decision—not just a feeling

Chapter 22

Understand Your Bond

"What God has joined together, let no one separate."

– Matthew 19:6

I believe in every good marriage there is a strength that you two have that is below the surface of the everyday things you do. It's something that sets you apart from others.

What is your strength?

Think about it… For example… my husband and I work together extremely well in time of need or emergency.

If there's an issue that needs solved and carried through… that's us! We get it done!

This isn't an everyday thing… sometimes not even a yearly thing but it seems to be our superpower… working together under pressure in times of chaos.

What is your superpower?

Take the time to find it.

Sometimes we are so in the middle of negativity in our relationship we can't see it.

Ask your partner their ideas on this.
Still can't figure it out.
Ask friends or parents… this list is endless.

Who knows you best- ask them. Why is this important to know… when things get hard… it's a good thing to reflect on. You'll need that strength to hold on too!

There will always be forces that try to drag you apart~ some of them people, some of them spiritual.

But you Can Not let that happen. Unite in a way that you both understand that Nothing will tear you apart.

Have a conversation about this exact topic. Discover your superpower as a couple.

God put you together therefore nothing shall put you under! This must be your motto!

We all have rainy days, but they make the sunny ones even brighter.

Always turn to each other in your time of need and learn to talk it out... No Matter what feelings you are having.

Just Stick Together!

"Love is patient, love is kind. It is not jealous, love is not pompous, it is not inflated, it is not rude, it does not seek its own interests, it is not quick-tempered, it does not brood over injury, it does not rejoice over wrongdoing but rejoices with the truth. It bears all things, believes all things, hopes all things, endures all things." 1 Corinthians 13:4-7

So, work together to understand that bond between you… discover the superpower in your relationship.

In your heart of hearts, would your spouse be your one support in all the chaos of life?

Yes, has to be the answer to this question.

If it’s not, someone has been sleeping through this relationship and needs to put in the work.

I’ve always said it takes two to tango- same goes for a good relationship.

You can’t be in it alone!

“Be devoted to one another in love. Honor one another above yourselves.” Romans 12:10

God Loves you and wants you to be Happily Married!

God Bless you and May He bring you peace in your hearts and in your marriages!

Marriage Takeaway:

- Identify your strength as a couple
- Lean on it during difficult times
- Protect your relationship from outside forces

Chapter 23

Bottling It Up

"Speak when you are angry, and you will make the best speech you will ever regret."

– Ambrose Bierce

The most destructive thing a person can do is hold things inside and not deal with them.

Things grow into uglier beings and fester into alien creatures this way. Yes, it comes bursting out as ugly as can be at the worst possible time.

Don't think this doesn't affect the entire family- it does!

This is where self-reflection can help in a big way!

Really get into why you react the way you do in any given situation.

Write down a situation and how you reacted to it. One you don't already understand your reaction to. Think about your childhood, school years, and past relationships. Dig deep!

Please take this time to truly understand yourself. Reflect through pray and times of silence.

Self-awareness and good coping skills will always be your friend in life and love.

Work together to get through all the variables of life.

Tell each other about all the ugly of your life and just be honest. It's the only ways to understand what your spouse is going through. Your partner wants to help you.

Talk about all of it!

Being vulnerable is a beautiful thing- not a weakness!

Those are the times your spouse truly understands your heart and soul and how much you trust them.

This is the one person you should not be afraid to be vulnerable with.

Let us open our hearts and ask God to help us in the times we are afraid to open up to our spouse and be totally vulnerable.

He will give you courage!

God bless you!

Marriage Takeaway:

- Don’t let things build up… talk them out
- Practice self-awareness and reflection
- Vulnerability builds deeper trust

Chapter 24

Honesty

"The truth may hurt for a little while,

but a lie hurts forever."

– Unknown

When you've been married a long time there are certain things you don't do or say because you know it's going to upset your spouse.

Oh! You've learned how to push those buttons, if you want too, but just stop yourself.

Self-control is something I use every day because there are so many snarky comments I'd love to make but I hold my tongue. It's just not productive!

This can be a defense mechanism that leads to suppressed feelings and dishonesty. Sometimes this even has you wanting to just toss the relationship out the window. At this point you can't seem to talk about anything. So, guess what needs to happen?

HONESTY!

You need to sit down, hash it all out and I mean everything from the past 20 years, lay it all on the table and deal with it.

It will be quite the load! Trust me I had to do just that.

After everything was said and we had it all on the table it allowed us to rebuild what we wanted in our relationship.

If you can survive that, you can succeed in marriage! It will make you a better couple! At first, you will both be amazed that you really held all that inside and still functioned in life.

But the end result, will be beautiful! Just be honest and don't make each other have to tip toe around things.

This is different than bringing up past issues during a regular argument about a present situation.

Issues that have built up over the years should be discussed at the appropriate time so your spouse can understand the deeper reason behind your feelings. That's very different from arguing about one isolated incident, like what happened at the Christmas party. I wanted to make this clarification in case there was any misunderstanding.

Be available and open to the communication that needs to happen. Your love desires to be honest and on fire with passion. How can this happen? Honesty!

May God find you in heated topics of honesty as often as possible!

God bless your heated conversations!

Marriage Takeaway:

- Be honest… even when it's uncomfortable
- Have the hard conversations
- Truth builds stronger relationships than silence

Chapter 25

What Does It Mean to Truly Love

"Love bears all things, believes all things,
hopes all things, endures all things."
– 1 Corinthians 13:7

Webster's online dictionary defines love as "a feeling of strong attachment induced by that which delight or commands admiration, devotion, and affection to one another."

But it is so much more than that!

Love is being vulnerable, trusting, and giving all of you to your spouse. When we do this, we become one with them.

So, is it really necessary to hide anything we are feeling, or things from our past not dealt with, and trying to protect ourselves from the judgement we all seem to dislike? No.

If you truly give yourself in your relationship, there should never be anything to hid or any dishonesty.

Be sacrificial to your spouse and always willing to do what is necessary for that love to grow and evolve into more.

God needs to be the center of your love.

If open and honest communication is your way of life, it allows you to grow through that relationship and evolve into a more spiritual couple with God's help and love.

Remember to pray together, for each other, and pray for peace in each other's hearts. This is an act of kindness that will shape your love!

Go with God in your heart, mind, and soul.
Love Him and He will love you!

Who am I kidding… He will love you anyway and patiently wait for you to love Him back!
The creator of love, does it best!

End note: This was a lot of fun to write! I do truly hope that it has helped you, even in some small way, to look at your relationship in a new light.

Reflect on your strengths as a couple and make note of some things you may need to improve on.

Remember to sacrifice, be kind, and honest with one another.

May God be with you in your marital bliss!

Marriage Takeaway:

- Love is action… not just a feeling
- Give yourself fully to your spouse
- Grow together spiritually and emotionally

The Wrap Up

Marriage isn't built in a day… and it certainly isn't fixed in 25.

But what you've just read isn't theory. It's not something pulled from a textbook. It's lived. It's tested. It's real.

Over these 25 days, you've seen the truth:
Marriage isn't complicated… people make it complicated.

It comes down to a few simple things:
Love each other.
Listen to each other.
Be honest with each other.
And never stop choosing each other.

Some days you'll get it right.
Some days you won't.

That's not failure… that's marriage.

What matters is that you keep showing up.
You keep trying.
You keep putting God at the center and each other right beside Him.

Because at the end of it all…
It’s not about perfection.

It’s about commitment.

It’s about growing old together… still laughing, still loving, still holding hands.

So don’t just read this book…

Live it.

One day at a time.

About The Author

Kim Anspach has been married to her husband, Rob, for over 37 years. Together, they've built a life centered around family, faith, and learning how to grow through every season of marriage.

They have raised six children, are now enjoying life with six grandchildren, and have shared their home with numerous pets along the way… each chapter bringing its own lessons, challenges, and plenty of laughter.

Kim is not a counselor or therapist, and she doesn't claim to have all the answers. What she does have is experience… real-life, day-to-day marriage experience that has been tested over time.

What began as a simple series of Facebook posts for friends turned into something more. Her honest, relatable thoughts about love, communication, and relationships struck a chord with others who were looking for something real… not perfect.

In addition to this book, Kim helped bring her grandmother's long-unpublished manuscript to life… honoring her legacy by contributing to its release and writing the foreword.

She has also partnered with her sister to create a line of all-natural products through Sisterly Scents, a venture rooted in care, creativity, and family.

Kim believes marriage doesn't have to be complicated. Through faith, patience, communication, and a willingness to keep showing up for one another, she believes any relationship can grow stronger.

Her hope is that this book encourages couples to laugh a little more, love a little deeper, and remember why they chose each other in the first place.

www.ingramcontent.com/pod-product-compliance
Lightning Source LLC
LaVergne TN
LVHW010929110826
845149LV00013B/2522

* 9 7 9 8 9 9 2 6 2 9 6 7 5 *